Fifty Sheds Of Grey

Three in a Shed

Also by C.T. Grey:

Fifty Sheds of Grey
Fifty Sheds Damper

Fifty Sheds Of Grey
Three in a Shed

C.T. Grey

BOXTREE

First published 2014 by Boxtree
an imprint of Pan Macmillan, a division of Macmillan Publishers Limited
Pan Macmillan, 20 New Wharf Road, London N1 9RR
Basingstoke and Oxford
Associated companies throughout the world
www.panmacmillan.com

ISBN 978-0-7522-6556-8

The picture acknowledgements on page 144 constitute
an extension of this copyright page.

1 3 5 7 9 8 6 4 2

A CIP catalogue record for this book is available from the British Library.

Designed and set by seagulls.net
Printed and bound in China

Visit **www.panmacmillan.com** to read more about all our books
and to buy them. You will also find features, author interviews and
news of any author events, and you can sign up for e-newsletters
so that you're always first to hear about our new releases.

To Charlotte for the foundations,
Dawn for the foliage and Sheldon
for the amusing water feature.

And now I stand alone in my garden, staring at the charred remains of my old shed. Just an empty shell. I puff out my cheeks and bite my lip. I thought I needed fifty shades of excitement in my life, but all I ever really needed was one shed of grey. My one true love. I smile and pick up my hammer.

'Come on, old girl,' I say. 'Let's get you fixed . . .'

Picture Acknowledgements

The following images are used under license from Shutterstock.com, 2014:

Pages 6 and 7 © Donjiy, 8 and 9 © kzww, 10 © Ulrich Mueller, 13 © Volker Rauch, 14 © millerium arkay, 16 and 17 © Tonis Valing, 18 © AdamEdwards, 21 © Chrislofotos, 22 and 23 © SunCity, 24 and 25 © Mikadun, 26 and 27 © Chuck Rausin, 29 © Maniola, 30 © natashamam, 33 © DJ Srki, 34 © Anne-Britt Svinnset, 36 and 37 © Steve Lovegrove, 38 and 39 ©Gualberto Becerra, 41 © Andrei Zveaghintev, 42 © Popkov, 45 © Zadiraka Evgenii, 46 © maturos 1812, 49 © Ekaterina Kamenetsky, 50 and 51 © Jiri Vaclavek, 52 and 53 © Anan Kaewkhammul, 54 and 55 © S_Photo, 56 and 57 © tobkatrina, 58 and 59 © Louise Sedgman Photographer, 60 © Rudy Umans, 63 © Masson, 64 © willmetts, 66 and 67 © Chrislofotos, 68 © kzww, 70 and 71 © Bobby Scrivener, 73 © Sally Scott, 74 © majeczka, 76 and 77 © Andrew Fletcher, 78 and 79 © STILLFX, 80 © E. Sweet, 83 © Denton Rumsey, 84 and 85 © Mark Blades, 87 © Chamille White, 88 © BrAt82, 91 © Alison Hancock, 92 © BONNIE WATTON, 95 © S_Photo, 96 and 97 © Flegere, 99 © Emily Veinglory, 100 © Marry Terriberry, 103 © Sukpaiboonwat, 104 and 105 © images 72, 107 © Adrian Zenz, 108 © TTphoto, 111 © Robyn Mackenzie, 112 and 113 © Kimmo Kesikinen, 115 © Anna Grigorjeva, 116 © Karen Grigoryan, 119 © Olivier Le Queinec, 120 © fotoduki, 122 and 123 © Marina Lohrbach, 124 © Egor Tetiushev, 127 © V. J. Matthew, 128 © brackish_nz, 130 and 131 © Uschi Hering, 132 © Darryl Sleath, 135 © Lester Balajadia, 136 and 137 © IxMaster, 138 and 139 © C.K.Ma, 141 ©Aleksey Stemmer, 142 © Michael Warwick.

I stand alone in my garden. How has it come to this? No women, no dignity and, worst of all, no shed!

Things were so different just a year ago, before I made a suggestion that would change my life for ever. A suggestion that would bring untold pleasure and untold pain . . .

'So . . .' I asked again, nervously, 'What do you think?'

I stared at Lady Christina and my estranged wife, Brenda. Lady Christina stared at me and Brenda. Brenda stared out of the window.

'It was just a thought,' I said, innocently. 'To keep everyone . . . happy? Kind of a ménage a trois? Or in this case, a cabane a trois.' I swept my arm around the shed to emphasize my point, as dramatically as I could with my arms still bound to the chair.

Finally someone replied.

'That's outrageous!' said Lady Christina. 'It's disgusting and immoral!' She paused. 'I like it.'

Brenda slowly turned her face from the window. It wore a startled, confused expression.

'You're honestly suggesting the three of us

. . . do it? Together? In here? How could we possibly do that?'

I scraped the sole of my shoe against the shed floor, like a naughty schoolboy. I'd had plenty of practice at that with Brenda.

'There's barely room for the two of us with all this junk in here!' she exclaimed.

I smiled with relief.

'Now you just call us when this shed is cleared out and not a moment sooner, do you hear?' she said, grabbing Lady Christina's arm and leading her to the door, 'And a touch of paint wouldn't go amiss. And some nice cushions. And a pair of curtains – we don't want the whole world knowing our business, now, do we? A nice floral pattern.'

The door shut. I stared around my shed and sighed. What had I got myself into? And how was I going to get out of the chair . . . ?

I couldn't believe I was in my shed with two women at the same time – I felt like a kid with a brand new train set. With two tunnels.

They asked me to smear their naked bodies with the produce from my herb garden, but I just couldn't do it. Too many women, not enough thyme.

'Prepare for pleasure beyond your wildest dreams!' they said, opening the shed door.

I gulped. 'You mean you've put a dartboard up?'

'So,' they asked,
perched provocatively
on my workbench,
'Do you know how
to make two women
happy at once?'

'Easy,' I said, and left.

'Come on,' they shouted eagerly. 'Prove you're a man!'

'All right, you asked for it,' I said, and left the finished toilet roll on the holder.

'How do you feel about using toys?' they asked.

'Great,' I said, 'But how are we going to fit the Scalextric in the shed?'

We finally agreed on the perfect position for a man and two women – me in the shed and them in the house watching *Emmerdale*.

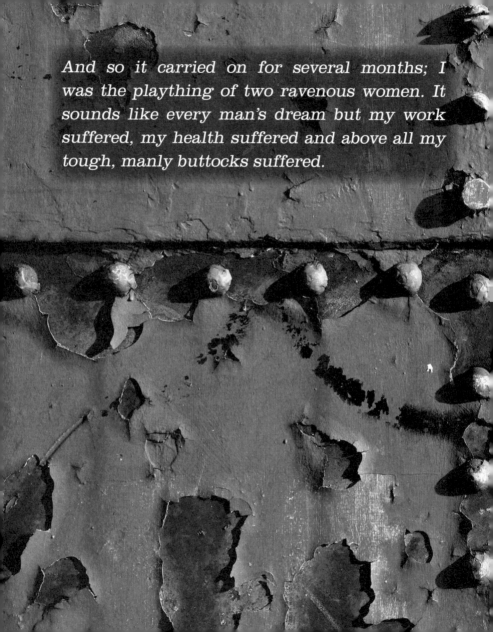

And so it carried on for several months; I was the plaything of two ravenous women. It sounds like every man's dream but my work suffered, my health suffered and above all my tough, manly buttocks suffered.

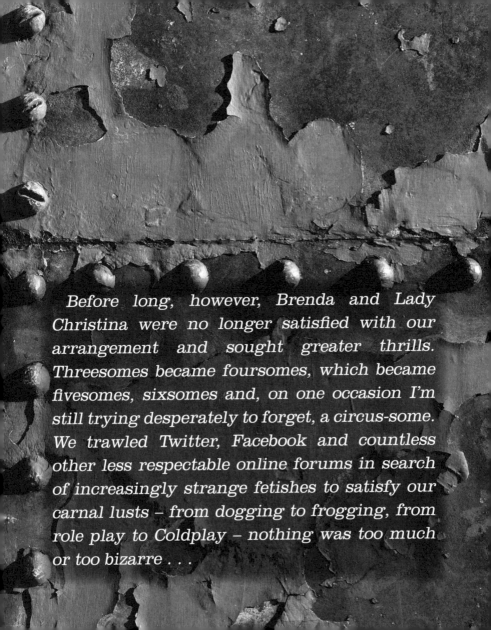

Before long, however, Brenda and Lady Christina were no longer satisfied with our arrangement and sought greater thrills. Threesomes became foursomes, which became fivesomes, sixsomes and, on one occasion I'm still trying desperately to forget, a circus-some. We trawled Twitter, Facebook and countless other less respectable online forums in search of increasingly strange fetishes to satisfy our carnal lusts – from dogging to frogging, from role play to Coldplay – nothing was too much or too bizarre . . .

'It's so long!' she squealed, 'I don't think you're going to fit it all in.'

'Sorry,' I sighed, 'Twitter only lets you write up to 140 characters.'

'Hold my wrists!' she begged, 'I need to be restrained!'

'All right,' I said, 'But wouldn't it be easier just to delete your Facebook account?'

'So,' she asked with an evil grin. 'Have you suffered enough yet?'

'Yes!' I cried desperately, 'Please, no more websites of kittens dressed as celebrities!'

Our bodies heaved and lurched
frantically against each other for
hours. It was the last time I got the
5.15 from Paddington.

'Mmmmm . . . you're so big!' she said, staring and licking her lips.

'Thank you,' I said, 'Although, to be fair, we are at Legoland.'

I was shocked when she stuffed her popcorn in my ears, into my nostrils and up my bottom. Turned out she was a sado-butterkist.

I pulled into the side
of the road and she
slowly slipped out of
her skintight catsuit,
unlaced her thigh-high
boots and peeled off her
long black gloves.

Then she put them all
back on again.

I'd only put 50p in the
parking meter.

'So,' she said, eyeing me up and down, 'Do you think a young man like you could satisfy a cougar?'

It was the last time I arranged an illicit rendezvous in a safari park.

We were shocked to be surrounded
by strange, sad-looking men,
staring through the car windows
and touching themselves. It was
the first time we'd been to the
International Motor Show.

I leant back against my workbench and asked her to do that thing Miley Cyrus does. So she brought her dad round to sing 'Achy Breaky Heart'.

I was delighted to see that soft, limp body begin to squirm wildly as it was pumped hard and fast. I'd never been to a Build-a-Bear before.

I'll never forget those long rubber boots, those fishnets and that exotic Scandinavian accent. It was the first time I'd ever been on a trawler.

We continued along this dark and bumpy road until one morning, while I was lying in bed recovering from a particularly exhausting trip to Seaworld, the phone rang . . .

'Hello, Mr Grey?' said a deep, female voice.

'Er . . . yes?' I answered, removing a piece of kelp from my ear.

'I just wondered if you'd care to comment on all the speculation?'

I frowned. 'Speculation?'

'Yes, Mr Grey,' came the brisk response. 'The speculation about who will play you?'

'Play me at what?'

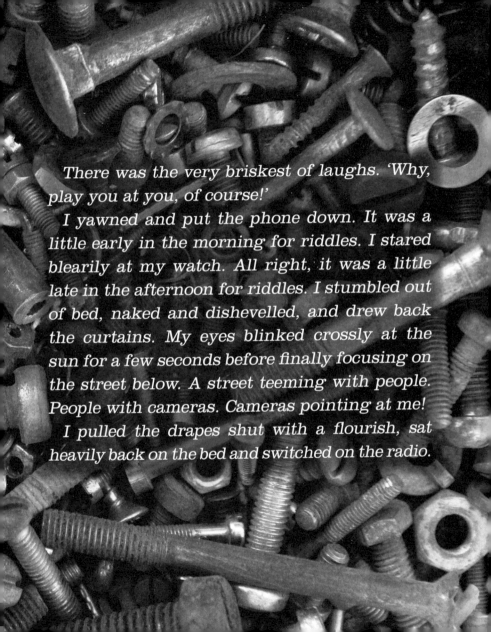

There was the very briskest of laughs. 'Why, play you at you, of course!'

I yawned and put the phone down. It was a little early in the morning for riddles. I stared blearily at my watch. All right, it was a little late in the afternoon for riddles. I stumbled out of bed, naked and dishevelled, and drew back the curtains. My eyes blinked crossly at the sun for a few seconds before finally focusing on the street below. A street teeming with people. People with cameras. Cameras pointing at me!

I pulled the drapes shut with a flourish, sat heavily back on the bed and switched on the radio.

'And in entertainment news, speculation continues to mount as to which Hollywood A-lister will be chosen to play the much sought-after role of multi-millionaire shed entrepreneur, erotic guru and three times winner of Shed of the Year (adult section) Colin Grey, in the upcoming film of his salacious and sordid life, *Fifty Sheds of Grey: The Movie*. The writers have insisted the lucky actor should have the charm of Pierce Brosnan, the body of Brad Pitt and the raw animal magnetism of Alan Titchmarsh. The search continues . . .'

I sat heavily back onto my seaweed-strewn bed. A film? But how? Who had written it? And why? I didn't want my 'salacious and sordid life' played out in front of millions of cinema-goers! As I lay there, my thoughts flitted about like a frantic moth before settling on a light bulb.

Wait, what was I thinking? All these theme park-based shenanigans must have dulled my keen business mind. They couldn't make any such film without my approval! All I had to do was take out an injunction and that would be the end of it. I sighed and closed my eyes. I'd go and see my solicitor in the morning and very soon this whole nightmare would be over . . .

So you see, there really is nothing to do, I'm afraid. They have a contract with your signature on it. They faxed me a copy. It's all there in black and white. And soon in technicolour.'

My solicitor pushed the sheet of paper across his large leather-topped desk towards me and steepled his fingers to his pursed lips.

I stared dumbfounded. It was my signature, all right – right down to the spade-shaped letter 'y'.

'But I don't understand,' I stammered. 'I don't remember signing this.'

My solicitor frowned.

'Are you saying you haven't signed any contracts recently?'

'Well, I . . . I mean, not in so much as . . . er . . . thank you, goodbye.'

I rushed out of the office. So that was it – every time you attended one of those 'special parties' you had to sign a contract, agreeing to whatever degrading practices might be available. Someone must have switched contracts. And now there was nothing I could do. Oh well, I would just have to hide from public view until it all blew over . . .

'Ladies and gentlemen, please welcome Brenda Grey, Lady Christina Mellors and the one and only Colin Grey!'

We walked down the red carpet, hand in hand . . . in hand, the paparazzi snapping away and the press thrusting oversized microphones under our noses. I sighed deeply. I hadn't remembered signing an agreement to attend the world premiere either. The cameras flashed. My companions lapped up the attention. Lady Christina was swathed in her family jewels and Brenda had had a special makeover for the occasion. And cosmetic surgery. Where was the woman I married? I sighed. Most of her was in a vat at the liposuction clinic.

After what seemed like hours, we were sitting down, the lights were dimming and the curtain was opening to reveal the Film Censorship Board's classification – a new one especially for this film – certificate 38.

'Here,' whispered Lady Christina, 'You'll need to put these on.'

'You mean, it's in 3D?!' I hissed.

'And Splash-o-rama,' said Brenda, drawing my attention to the numerous small sprinklers placed strategically around the theatre.

I gulped and sank as low as possible into my seat. I wished it would swallow me up, but then stopped wishing, in case that was another available feature.

The film opened on a shot of Lady Christina's huge landscaped garden. The garden where it all began so many years ago. Where a sophisticated older woman took an innocent young man under her wing. And on the patio. And in the shrubbery. I shuffled uncomfortably as the scenes played out before me on the giant screen . . .

Her eyes were cold, her eyes were deep. Her eyes were the kind of eyes a man could easily get lost in. Like IKEA.

She gasped as it became harder and stiffer the moment she touched it. I probably should have warned her about that quick-set cement.

'Let me take a closer look at your manhood,' she said, slowly pulling down the zip.

'OK,' I replied, 'But technically it's called a cagoule.'

She said she wanted to try the wheelbarrow position. So I leant her against the fence by the compost heap.

'You make my panties so wet!' she squirmed.

'Don't blame me,' I said, 'You should've taken them off the line before I turned on the sprinkler.'

'I'll do whatever you want,'
she said. Before long she was
drenched in sweat and panting
desperately. She obviously hadn't
done much digging before.

PLEASE
KEEP OFF THE
GRASS

As we rolled and heaved desperately, we knew what we were doing was wrong. We'd both seen the Keep Off The Grass sign.

Despite being an attractive older woman, she didn't like me calling her a Mother I'd Like to Do Everything With. Or MILDEW, for short.

Her whole body bucked and heaved as she felt a hot throbbing between her legs. It was the last time she ever went on my ride-on lawnmower.

'Mmmmm,' she said, stroking my giant rhubarb, 'This is big enough to win first prize at the county fair.'

'I know,' I said, 'But I'm a grower not a shower.'

The audience was hushed. I glanced round at their open-mouthed faces, their eyes alternating between the screen and me. I tried to hide behind my tub of popcorn, wishing I'd gone for the extra-large after all. Brenda elbowed me playfully as the scenes from our marriage began. A marriage which had been perfectly happy and relatively normal until she bought THAT book . . .

'I need a real man and I need him now!' she cried.

'Here I am,' I said eagerly.

'Good,' she smiled, 'Now, get the top off this pickle jar.'

The bed shook, creaked and rattled as she gripped the headboard and screamed out my name.

At this point we were asked to leave Debenhams.

'Are you ready
to be tortured
in a way only
a woman can
torture a man?'
she asked.

I nodded
nervously.

'All right,' she
said, and ate
half my chips.

Frantically I tore off her dress,
her bra and her lacy knickers.
My heart was in my mouth,
but I just managed to close the
wardrobe before she got home.

'I've been such a bad girl,' she said,
leaning up against the shed wall.
'I deserve to be punished.'

'Very well,' I said, and cancelled
her credit card.

When it was fully erect she got on, jerking up and down wildly.

'That's great,' I said, 'But shouldn't we let the kids go on the bouncy castle first?'

'Now, which whip shall it be today?'
she teased, licking her lips.

'I don't know,' I said, 'I just can't
decide between banana and
butterscotch.'

She leant over the kitchen table.
'Smack that bottom,' she squealed,
'Smack it hard!'

'I am,' I said, 'But the ketchup just
won't come out.'

We had the
perfect 24-hour
sadomasochistic
relationship.

I snored all night
and she moaned
about it all day.

'Go on, I'll let you stick it in there,' she sighed, 'As it's your birthday.'

I grinned. It wasn't every day I was allowed to have the plasma TV in the shed.

As I lay there on the floor, my naked body covered in treacle and whipped cream, I heard those inevitable words . . . 'Clean up on aisle 3.'

She said she liked it doggy style so I
threw her a stick. Still waiting . . .

The seasons flew by on the cinema screen.
Spring, summer, autumn and now winter . . .

Her body trembled and shook. 'I can't wait any longer, do it now!' she cried.

'OK,' I said, and got the winter duvet from the airing cupboard.

I slowly opened the door to see a woman dressed head to toe in leather and brandishing a whip. It was the last time I bought an advent calendar from Ann Summers.

'I feel so hot,' she cried, 'My whole body's tingling!'

'I know,' I said, 'I told you not to get a onesie from the market.'

'Do it,' she begged.

'OK,' I said, tying her hands and gagging her, 'But there must be easier ways to avoid putting on weight at Christmas.'

'Hurt me,' she begged, leaning over the dining table expectantly.

'OK,' I replied, 'Your turkey's too dry and your sprouts are overcooked.'

She said she was turned on by men who lived dangerously. So I bought her present from the 24-hour garage on Christmas Eve.

'That's so hot,' she cried, 'It feels so good inside me.'

I smiled smugly. You can't beat a steaming mug of Bovril on a cold winter's night.

I sighed as I felt the hot breath on my neck and that hungry tongue licking my face. I should never have asked for a puppy for Christmas.

I find myself smiling and shake myself. It wasn't all perfect. I was looking back through rose-coloured 3D glasses. As the later scenes of our marriage showed . . .

'I'll do anything you wish!' she cried as she stood naked before me.

'OK,' I said, 'Could you move to the left a bit? I can't see *Match of the Day*.'

I accidentally mixed up my Viagra with my hearing aid. Now I've got a hard of hearing on.

'Bend over and do exactly what I say,' she ordered.

I shuddered as she pulled on the long rubber gloves and squeezed the thick liquid from the tube.

'OK,' she said, 'This is how you do the washing up . . . '

I put her over my
knee and before long
the shed was shaking
with howls of pain.

Damn my arthritis.

'I'm desperate for a man's touch in the bedroom,' she begged.

So I left my socks on the floor and my pants on the bedside lamp.

She took a deep breath as I forced myself in. No doubt about it – if I didn't lose weight soon, I'd need to get a bigger shed.

After two long hours it was suddenly over. No threesome, no kidnapping nor any of the events of recent years. At least I had been spared that embarrassment! I peered out from behind my fingers in time to see the credits. And one caught my eye – 'Screenplay by Lady Christina Mellors and Brenda Grey'! And another – 'Part Two of the Fifty Sheds Trilogy Coming to a Theatre Near You Soon'!

I sighed wistfully. Things used to be so uncomplicated. Just a man and his wife. And her whip and handcuffs.

'We need to talk,' said Lady Christina, after the long, silent journey home.

'Oh, right,' I said, opening the shed door.

'Where are you going?' asked Brenda, closing it again.

'You said you needed to talk,' I said.

'We need to talk to you,' said Lady Christina.

'Oh, OK,' I said, sitting down on a bag of cement.

'We betrayed your trust,' said Brenda, 'And we're sorry. Rich . . . but sorry. And we've come to a decision – we need some time to ourselves. It's not you, it's us.'

'You mean, like a trial separation?'

'Yes,' said Lady Christina, 'A trial separation. A permanent one.'

I gulped. 'But you know you're the only two for me.'

'We're sorry,' said Brenda. 'We'll deal with the media. We'll say it's a conscious untripling.'

'But I got candles!' I blurted, urgently lighting one. 'Sandalwood . . . or cedarwood . . . I'm not really sure, but I've definitely got some kind of wood and I don't want to waste it!'

'We know you have, dear,' said Lady Christina, placing a long, perfectly manicured finger over my quivering lips. 'Now just calm down. You must have known it wouldn't last. These things never do.'

'Yes,' said Brenda, 'If we hadn't ended it, you would have done, sooner or later. At the end of the day, neither of us could possibly compete with your true love.'

'My true love?' I whispered as I watched them walk out of the door, out of my garden and out of my life.

I stood still in the middle of my shed, numb and alone, my face solemn in the candlelight, then shot out of the shed in time to see them walk off into the sunset together. I breathed in deeply and sadly, taking in the sweet perfume of honeysuckle and the smokey scent of . . . smoke?

I frowned for a moment then swivelled round sharply.

I stared in horror. In my haste, I must have knocked over one of the candles. My shed was on fire! And not with sweaty, kinky passion.

I grabbed my garden hose in both hands, pointed it at the blaze and frantically squirted for all I was worth. The flames licked at the tip but I sprayed on regardless. After what seemed like hours, but was in fact only a few minutes, I collapsed onto the crazy paving, and rolled over exhausted and completely spent . . .